Starting Your North Carolina LLC

Second Edition

Richard Wayne Bobholz

ISBN-10: 0-9977338-6-1
ISBN-13: 978-0-9977338-6-0

DEDICATION

This book is dedicated to those clients that have helped make its creation possible. Thanks to those earlier clients who gave a new attorney a chance, and thanks to those clients who believed in what Law Plus Plus is aiming to do. Without all our clients, Law++ would not be a success, and we wouldn't be able to enact the change we seek in the legal system.

CONTENTS

INTRODUCTION

If you're reading this, you're likely planning on forming a North Carolina Limited Liability Company. I'm very excited for you, as that's a huge step towards legitimizing your business.

This is the second edition of this book. It was updated to reflect many changes in the law and a major change in the Secretary of State's articles of organization template. What you will find in this guidebook is the most up-to-date information regarding the process of forming your LLC at the time this guide was published.

I got into the business of law because I enjoy helping other people. I especially enjoy helping people start and maintain their companies. This book aims to help a larger audience than I can reach in my day-to-day. If you have questions above and beyond what this book can answer, please feel free to reach out to me at richard@lawplusplus.com. I'll answer whatever I can, but be aware that I receive hundreds of emails every day, and it may be a couple of days before I can reply.

As we lawyers do, I must also give you a couple of disclaimers. First of all, all the information in this book is educational and informational in nature. Because I do not know your specific facts, I cannot give you any sort of legal advice, and this book should not be taken as such.

Second, nothing written in this book is meant to establish an attorney-client relationship. I'd be more than happy to discuss that possibility, but there is no relationship of that nature until an engagement letter is signed by both you and I. This limitation includes any details you send me. If you'd like to discuss hiring me, please say that in your email.

Third, if you do choose to contact me, please keep the inquires specific as to who you are, but general about all other facts. This is because lawyers have conflicts of interest, and I must ensure that I do not gain information from you that could help or harm one of my current clients. Here's an example:

> Hi Richard. My name is Joan of Arc. I'm starting a company called The French Revolution, a bakery that I'm starting in Winston Salem. I wanted to know if you'd be able to help me decide between a couple of terms I want to include in my Operating Agreement? Thank you, Joan.

Finally, laws change, circumstances change, and your situation is likely unique. Because of this, I cannot guarantee everything in this book will be useful (or even not harmful) in your situation. I know you're a smart person and can use independent judgment when deciding what is right for your situation.

Many times, throughout this book, I use the word "default." When I use this term, it means that this is what automatically happens if you do not take some action to change it. Most things that are default can be changed by you.

About Law Plus Plus

Law Plus Plus is a revolutionary new type of law firm where we analyze the best way to operate a law firm for the benefit of our business clients. Our analysis has lead us to the creation of almost 100% flat rate fees, easy to understand policies, monthly subscriptions, business development help, and much more.

For more on Law++, check out www.lawplusplus.com.

Questions? Comments? Feedback? Requests for other books? Feel free to email me at richard@lawplusplus.com.

CHAPTER 1
CHOICE OF ENTITY

So, you're about to start a company in North Carolina? Congratulations! Starting a company is an exciting adventure. It is a lot of work, but your hard work makes it worth it in the end.

At this point, in your startup process, I'm assuming you have some sort of plan. You should already know where this venture is headed, and you should know what your goals are. Whatever your goals, at this point, it is vital to have them.

Before we start, always remember that if set up properly, it isn't that difficult to switch between entity types, but it will cost you a minimum of the state filing fee for a new entity, plus whatever other expenses you'll incur.

There are five main choices for entity type:

1. Sole Proprietorship
2. Partnership
3. Limited Partnership
4. Limited Liability Company (LLC)
5. C Corporation

You've probably heard of a few, if not all, of these. I've placed them in this order because it is how I view the spectrum of liability and formality. I typically start at the top and decide if that is an appropriate fit or not. If it isn't, I move to the next, stopping only when I feel that structure is appropriate for the particular company I'm working with. We will do the same here. Realistically, I start at LLC and choose between that and corporation as the other choices make sense in extremely rare circumstances.

Sole Proprietorship

A sole proprietorship is what you have if you just start a business, by yourself, without filing any papers with the state. There's no filing requirement outside of any necessary business licenses for specific business activities. There are also no additional tax formalities. Certain ordinary business deductions can be made on your personal 1040 and all revenue is reported as wages. In North Carolina, these earnings and deductions would be reported on your D-400 tax form.

As a sole proprietor, you must also withhold your self-employment tax, which includes both halves of the FICA tax. This rate is 15.3% of your income. You are entitled to a deduction on your income taxes for the 7.65% of the FICA that is attributed to the business side.

What is most concerning about sole proprietorships is the fact that they subject the owner to unlimited personal liability. Because the business and the owner are one in the same, any debts or wrongdoings of the company are debts and wrongdoings of the owner. Even with an otherwise amazing asset protection plan, this is not a good position to be in.

Partnership

Also called a general partnership, a partnership is the entity that is formed when you start a business with multiple people as owners with no entity filed with the state. Partnerships do not require filings with the state nor do they require annual reports. This structure still requires necessary business licenses to be obtained.

General partnerships are owned and controlled equally by each partner, absent an agreement that states otherwise. Because any one partner can control the company and make it do whatever that partner wants, it is very important to have a partnership agreement in place before you begin operations.

Partnerships are merely a collection of people, meaning that the partnership of Bobholz, O'Brien, and Smith is just the collective efforts of Bobholz, O'Brien, and Smith. If Smith were to pass away, the partnership would die with him. What each partner owns is an equal share of the assets and profits of the company. There's no stock, nor any way to sell a partnership share without a partnership agreement stating otherwise.

As mentioned, partnerships should have partnership agreements prior to engaging in business together. This is a document that outlines how the company is to be run, how ownership is distributed, how earnings are distributed, and all the other very important details that should be discussed prior to entering into a partnership. Absent a partnership agreement, the terms are determined by the default rules in the North Carolina Uniform Partnership Act under Chapter 59 of the North Carolina General Statutes. These default rules are lacking very important terms.

For taxes, there is a slight increase in the amount of paper work, but no additional tax to pay. You are once again taxed individually on your 1040, but your partnership is required to submit form 1065 to the IRS. In North Carolina, your partnership is required to fill out form D-403. Partners are taxed on their share of the partnership profits. Even money that is earned by the partnership, yet not distributed to the partners is taxed individually. If your company earns money for years without paying the owners, the owners are still liable for tax on that income.

The FICA tax is worth addressing, even though the

outcome remains the same as it would be in a sole proprietorship. The amount each partner earns is taxed at 7.65%. A partner is deemed to have earned the income as soon as the partnership does regardless of if he or she receives any personal income, granted the net income of the partnership is only calculated at the end of the year. On top of the individual share, the partner would have to pay 7.65% of his or her share of the income. Since a partner is deemed to own only an equal share of the assets, profits and losses, this calculation looks very similar to the sole proprietorship.

As is similar to that of a sole proprietorship, there is unlimited liability for a partnership. This means that any debt or wrongdoing by one partner can cause the other partners to get sued personally. The partner or partners who get sued may always sue the wrongdoer for contribution to repay them, but that only works if the wrongdoer is able to be found and has enough assets to cover the expense. The cost of having to go to court is also very expensive

Limited Partnership (LP)

A limited partnership is similar to a partnership except the limited partners have no personal liability for the debts or actions of the partnership. Only the general partner or partners can be held personally liable; however, only the general partner or partners can manage the company. A general partner can be a corporation or LLC, but that asks the question: Why not just form an LLC or corporation?

With the advent of Limited Liability Companies, these Limited Partnerships have significantly decreased in numbers, since they require a filing with the state, retain some liability in the general partner, and are not as flexible with member/partner rights as an LLC.

Limited Liability Company (LLC)

The limited liability company (LLC) is, by far, the most popular choice recently in North Carolina. We will spend a fair bit of time discussing what makes LLCs so popular. The LLC isn't the best for all circumstances, but it is very flexible, tax neutral, and has limited liability for the members.

One of the most useful aspects of an LLC in North Carolina is the choice of how it is taxed. Because of the advantages of the partnership "pass-through" taxation, most choose that route so they are taxed only once as the income is earned. If you have an LLC with only one member, your LLC is treated as a disregarded entity for federal taxation purposes. This just means it is treated like a sole proprietorship instead of a partnership for taxation only. If taxed as a partnership, you will have to file form 1065 annually with the IRS and form D-403 for North Carolina. Each individual member will have to fill out his or her share on his or her 1040 and D-400. If the LLC is treated as a disregarded entity, everything will go on your individual 1040 and D-400.

For self-employment or FICA taxes, the net taxes remain the same as if you were a sole proprietor for single member LLCs and the same as a partnership for pass through LLCs.

To form an LLC, you must file your articles of organization with the North Carolina Department of the Secretary of State and wait about a week for your certificate of organization in the mail. LLCs can have a name separate from its owners, so long as that name does not contain any of the reserved words and it includes some variation or abbreviation of "limited liability company."

Your company's name also cannot be the same or very similar name as another company in North Carolina, nor can the name suggest that the company performs a function that it does not. I could not name my law office

"The Medical office of George Washington" because I do not perform medical services and I unfortunately cannot claim to be affiliated with George Washington. The cost for filing is $125 at the time I wrote this book. As with all entities, any required business licenses must be obtained prior to starting operations. With an LLC, you must also obtain an EIN from the IRS so that your company has a distinct identification number when opening bank accounts and filing taxes.

In order to maintain the LLC's active status, a few important formalities must be followed. First, an annual report must be filed every year with the state. This is a very simple form that asks for general information about your company, officers, and registered agent. Along with the annual report, you must also pay a $200 fee.

The second formality is maintaining the distinct nature of the LLC. This means that you have to operate as though you were caring for someone else's stuff, even if you're the only member. You can do this by writing letters authorizing you to do any action and signing as manager or however your LLC treats management.

You must also maintain separate bank accounts, with no comingling of funds with your personal accounts. As soon as you use the business debit card to buy groceries, you put yourself at risk of ruining the limited liability nature of the LLC.

Third, but not least, you must keep good records. All of your transactions and company decisions should be written down and stored. The formalities take getting used to. After they become instinctual, they make a lot of sense.

As long as you've followed the formalities and didn't do anything to bring liability on you personally, you will enjoy the limited liability protection of the LLC. No member can be automatically liable for the debts or wrongdoings of the LLC, its employees, or its members. LLC ownership cannot be taken by creditors of a member. This is a big difference between LLCs and Corporations where the stocks are assets available to the creditors. What the creditors can receive from the LLC member is what is called a charging order, which only allows the creditor to receive income payments that would have gone to the member who owes the creditor.

The LLC is owned by members and the ownership interest can be divided up however the members choose. Without an agreement otherwise, we would look to the North Carolina statutes to see who receives what interest amount. I would always recommend writing up an operating agreement when writing the articles of organization. Even a simple agreement goes a long ways for resolving disputes down the road. We cover operating agreements in a few chapters.

Another good part about LLCs is that membership can be bought, sold, traded, defined, inherited or transferred in nearly any way. Since they are so flexible, you may also create different types of membership. This is beneficial if the members want to raise capital but do not want to give up any control of the company. If the investor will agree, it is a nice strategy to have available. For many reasons, investors shy away from LLCs, preferring the C Corporation instead. Most important of these reasons is that the partnership tax treatment is a disadvantage to investors.

Under North Carolina law, since 2014, members are managers of the company by default. This can be changed in the LLC's operating agreement to have a single manager, group of managers, board of managers or any other setup that (1) has at least one manager, and (2) does not infringe on the guaranteed rights of the other members.

C Corporation (C Corp)

The C corporation is the traditional vehicle for investment-backed companies or companies with ever changing ownership. Although an LLC can operate in much the same way, the C corporation has a more defined delineation between owners and management. This leads to many distinct structural and tax differences.

To form a C corporation, you must file articles of incorporation with the North Carolina Department of the Secretary of State, file for an EIN through the IRS, and pay $125. The shareholders must also elect board members to control the company and adopt bylaws to set the rules for how the company will operate.

C corporations are completely distinct from their owners. This means these entities are taxed separately. They must file form 1120 with the IRS annually, and in North Carolina, they file form CD-405. What is unpleasant about the C corporation is how distributions to the owners are taxed. Because dividends are not deductible, there is a "double tax" on the amount the corporation pays in dividends. First, that income is taxed at the corporate level when it is earned. The shareholder's dividend income is then taxed again on each individual's 1040. Of course, you can pay workers a salary to avoid this double tax effect because wages are deductible from the corporate tax. Wages must be paid reasonably for actual work done, and wages are subject to both income and FICA taxes. You'll likely pay less in total taxes as income versus dividends; however, that depends on your personal situation.

It is possible to have no earned income and only receive dividend income, which is not subject to FICA taxes. If you work for the corporation and receive wages, you will pay your 7.65% and the corporation will pay its 7.65% of your income. This is the FICA tax.

With all the other entities, when the company earns profit, the owners must report the income on their 1040s regardless of if they were paid. Those other types of companies could not hold onto large amounts of cash without forcing their owners to pay tax on income they had not received. A corporation is subject to its own taxation, so while it doesn't make distributions to its shareholders, its shareholders are not taxed. The stored money, however, can be taxed at the dividend rate if there is no legitimate reason to be storing up that money. This would lead to a "triple tax" situation, so it is best to ensure there is always a legitimate business reason when storing up money in a corporation. Some companies store billions while using the justification that they may buy out competitors in the future, so there are plenty of legitimate reasons to keep large stores of money on hand.

The owners of a C corporation are the shareholders or stockholders. In a C corporation, shareholders can be people from any nation, companies, trusts, or any other entity that is allowed to own assets in the United States. With no restrictions on who may own the shares, there is a much larger pool of potential investors available to a C corporation than to an entity taxed as an S corporation, and with the stock markets, they are much easier to find than an LLC.

Owners in a corporation hold onto a portion of the company in devices called shares. Ownership of shares entitles a person to certain rights in the company, depending on the bylaws, stock purchase agreement, or other contracts associated with the purchase or acquisition of the shares. There are also state and federal laws that provide rights and responsibilities to shareholders. Most shares come with the right to vote for the board of directors. Shareholders also typically have some say in matters like changes to the bylaws, a sale of the company, or whether to dissolve the company.

The board of directors in a corporation appoints the

management of the company. The most iconic example of the management is the chief executive officer, or CEO for short. The management then runs the day-to-day operations of the company.

The formalities of a C corporation are the strictest of all the choices. You must keep assets separate. You must have bylaws and articles and abide by them. A C corporation must have an annual meeting of the shareholders where they may vote on things like new directors or changes to the bylaws. Meeting minutes must be kept for the annual meeting and all other meetings. An annual report must also be filed each year with the Secretary of State. If the C corporation wants to be publicly traded, there are significantly more formalities and filing obligations through the state of North Carolina and through the SEC. Up until the point when you go public, these formalities, although rigid, are not too tough to follow. You're obligated to follow them, but they also help keep your company organized.

S Corporation (S Corp)

An S corporation is a tax election for corporations or LLCs. An S corporation is a hybrid between the partnership and corporation taxations. To qualify, the company must only have one class of stock, have one hundred or fewer shareholders, have no non-natural persons as shareholders, have only US citizens as shareholders, and the profits and losses must be proportional to each shareholder's interest in the company.

The benefit of this election is the elimination of FICA taxes on some of your income. The disadvantage is the increased cost of compliance. To elect to be taxed as an S corporation, you must file form 2553 with the IRS in the first 3 ½ months of any tax year.

CHAPTER 2
TREATMENT OF STARTUP FUNDS

Sometimes a small concept can make a huge difference. Because of the difference between LLCs and corporations, the money you put in to start them is treated in very different ways.

Startup Funds

Corporation – When you put money into a corporation, you are investing in exchange for shares. Generally, you only contribute money in exchange for new shares, but although not advisable, you can structure this differently. Because you're exchanging money for shares, you can only recoup the money you've contributed when you dispose of the shares, either selling them to a third party or to the company. Any income you receive that is not in exchange for shares would be reported as ordinary income or dividends. When you sell your shares, the portion equal to the amount you paid will be return on capital and all gains would be capital gains.

Corporations are great for growing the company and making most of your money solely from the sale of the company. Stock options in exchange for labor or stock in exchange for labor will have a vastly different tax treatment than a pure investment.

For example, if you contribute $100,000 for 100,000 shares, each share is worth $1. If you get paid $50,000 the first year, but retain all of your shares, you pay income tax on the $50,000. On the other hand, if you sell back 50,000 shares in exchange for $50,000, you will pay no taxes, as it will likely all be considered return on capital. If you sell back 10,000 shares in exchange for $50,000, the $40,000 gain would likely be considered capital gains for tax purposes and $10,000 would likely be considered return on capital. Be careful with this, however, because your company's valuation will affect these things. You cannot completely avoid income tax by trading your stock back, but if your company's value has increased significantly since you received your shares, it may be reasonable for the income to be capital gains opposed to income tax. Talk to a CPA or tax attorney before trying this strategy.

Limited Liability Company – LLCs can be taxed as a disregarded entity, partnership, S corporation, or C corporation. The default of a multimember LLC is partnership. When you put money into an LLC that is taxed as a partnership, you are investing in exchange for equity. Under partnership taxation, this increases your capital account. When the LLC has profit, you increase your capital account as well. You're subject to income and FICA tax on only the amount you're liable for when the LLC has profits, not when you're paid. When you get your investment paid back is somewhat up to you. Since you're only taxed on profits in most companies, this realized tax savings happens right away with the expenses your investment was spent on. In LLCs with multiple members, this analysis can become vastly more complicated.

For example, if you invest $100,000 in your LLC and you're the sole owner (100%), and your LLC makes $50,000 the first year. If you pay yourself $50,000, you pay income tax on the entire $50,000. If you pay yourself $60,000, you're only subject to income tax on the first $50,000 and the $10,000 would be return on capital.

Conclusion

LLCs can give you your return on capital faster as the company grows and is able to support itself whereas you must sell your shares of the corporation in order to take advantage of the return on capital tax treatment of corporate stock. These two different ways of handling taxation and investment may make the difference between forming a corporation or forming a limited liability company. The tax treatment of startup funds is only one part of the equation.

CHAPTER 3
LLC FORMATION INTRO

To form your company, you will need to file the articles of incorporation or organization with the entity tasked with forming companies in your state. Each state is different, but in North Carolina, this is the Department of the Secretary of State. Fortunately, the NC Secretary of State's website includes article templates that you can print and complete in order to complete your formation.

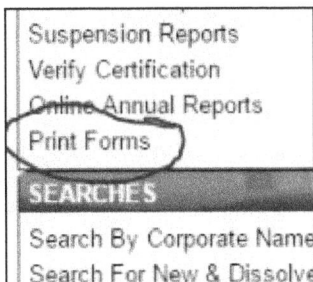

LLC Article Parts

For your LLC, there are actually very few required terms for your company's articles of organization. The most common parts are:

Name of the Company. (Required) You name must include "LLC," "Limited Liability Company," or any other common abbreviation for a limited liability company. Before choosing a name, you should also run through a name search, checking the Secretary of State's site, the USPTO, register of deeds, Google, domain registry, and any state trademark offices in which you might want to conduct business.

Registered Agent and Address. (Required) This is the person or entity that is located within the state that is responsible for accepting service of process on behalf of the company. This is important because this is the place a person can sue a business in the event the business has wronged that person. Just by serving this person, even if the business owner never gets the lawsuit, the business is deemed on notice and the court has jurisdiction over the company.

Principal Office Location. This isn't required in North Carolina for LLCs, but it provides a backup for the registered agent in case service cannot be obtained on the registered agent. It also provides the public with more information about your company. If service is missed, the plaintiff may serve the Secretary of State instead of your company, and the Secretary of State will dissolve the company if they cannot get that service to you.

Member Managed versus Manager Managed. In NC, all members are managers automatically unless the articles or operating agreement specify otherwise. Older articles used to include this difference; however, it is now common practice to only include this information in your operating agreement, not in your articles.

Organizer (Required). The organizer does not necessarily have to be a member, but the organizer is the person who is setting up the LLC. This person has only the authority to set up the LLC, unless the articles or operating agreement specify that he or she is a member or manager.

CHAPTER 4
STEP BY STEP LLC
FORMATION

We live in a DIY society, where everyone has some sort of do-it-yourself project going on somewhere. We find that when it comes to setting up your business, this still holds true. A lot of people we work with are setting up their own business structures with limited setback. Especially if you're on your own or have a very small company, the DIY route can have little to no risk.

If people are going to go the DIY route anyway, we want to provide the best resources possible to eliminate as much risk as we can. (Keep in mind there is a complex analysis around choosing between an LLC, Corporation or other type of legal entity. Choosing the wrong type may have unintended liability or tax consequences.)

Step 1: What's in a name?

A rose by any other name would smell as sweet, right? When you're picking your name, you may want to consult family, friends, and branding experts to discuss what name or names would best fit your business idea. There are two general types of names: descriptive and creative. 'Google' is a good example of creative, and 'R. W. Bobholz Law, PLLC' is a good example of descriptive. As their names suggest, a descriptive name gives the audience a sense of what the company does whereas a creative name does not.

Step 2: Search for your name.

Once you've decided on a name, you're going to have to search the Secretary of State database to make sure the name isn't taken. Additionally, you should search the uspto.gov trademark database to ensure that you're not violating someone's trademark by using this name. Lastly, if you plan on having a website or any web presence, you should make sure that your domain name is available, preferably in a .com top level domain.

Secretary of State

Search: http://www.sosnc.gov/search/index/corp

Division:

| Corporations ⌄ |

Search For:

| Corporations ⌄ |

Choose A Search Type:

| Name Starting With ⌄ |

Organizational Name: ⓘ

| |

| Search |

USPTO Trademark

Go to www.uspto.gov and search for your name to ensure you're not infringing on anyone else's trademark. You will need to not only search your company's name exactly as spelled, but also spelling variations and stylistic variations. The standard for trademarks is "likelihood of confusion," so an exact match isn't necessary to infringe on someone else's mark.

Fortunately, these trademarks are only good in specific industries. If someone has your desired name trademarked, but they're in a distinct industry, you're not likely to infringe on their rights.

Trademarks is a very complicated area of law, so if there is any doubt, you should speak with an attorney.

While you're searching, you should also search the state trademark office of any state you intend to do business in.

Domain

Using your favorite domain registrar, search for your desired domain to ensure it isn't taken.

Step 3: Download the Articles of Organization

In order to create a legal entity, you must file articles of organization with the Secretary of State's office here in North Carolina. This is an easy process that starts with downloading the empty articles of organization here or by using the QR code:
http://www.sosnc.gov/corporations/forms.aspx?PItemId=5429715&Type=LimitedLiability%20Company

I personally prefer the .doc version over the .pdf version. My preference is based largely on ease in which I can make changes. Both are equally valid when filed with the Secretary of State. To download the .doc version, you have to click the document icon in the second column.

Step 4: Fill in the Articles

[Sample as of May 14, 2017]

State of North Carolina
Department of the Secretary of State
Limited Liability Company
ARTICLES OF ORGANIZATION

Pursuant to §57D-2-20 of the General Statutes of North Carolina, the undersigned does hereby submit these Articles of Organization for the purpose of forming a limited liability company.

1. The name of the limited liability company is:
2. The name and address of each person executing these articles of organization is as follows: (State whether each person is executing these articles of organization in the capacity of a member, organizer, or both.

   Note: This document must be signed by all persons listed.)

Name	Address	Capacity
_____	_____	_____
_____	_____	_____
_____	_____	_____

3. The name of the initial registered agent is:
   _____

4. The street address and county of the initial registered agent office of the limited liability company is:

   Number and Street_____

   City_____ State: NC Zip Code: _____

   County:_____

5. The mailing address, if different from the street address, of the initial registered agent office is:

   Number and Street_____

   City_____ State: NC Zip Code_____

   County:_____

6. Principal office information: (Select either a or b.)

a. ☐ The limited liability company has a principal office.

The principal office telephone number: _____

The street address and county of the principal office of the limited liability company is:

Number and Street:

_____

City: _____ State: _____
Zip Code: _____County: _____

The mailing address, if different from the street address, of the principal office of the company is:
Number and Street:

_____

City: _____ State: _____
Zip Code: _____County: _____

b. ☐ The limited liability company does not have a principal office.

7. Any other provisions which the limited liability company elects to include (e.g., the purpose of the entity) are attached.

8. (**Optional**): Listing of Company Officials (See instructions on the importance of listing the company officials in the creation document.

Name	Title	Business Address

9. (**Optional**): Please provide a business e-mail address:

_____

The Secretary of State's Office will e-mail the business automatically at the address provided above at no cost when a document is filed. The e-mail provided will not be viewable on the website. For more information on why this service is offered, please see the instructions for this document.

10. These articles will be effective upon filing, unless a future date is specified:

This is the _____day of _____, 20__.

_____

_____
Signature

_____
Type or Print Name and Title

You'll notice the form is very simple. Completing the form isn't the hard part of forming a new company.

Name: Your name must be unique, not in violation of someone's trademark, not contain certain reserved words like engineer, lawyer, architect, etc. without board approval, and must contain some variation or abbreviation of "limited liability company."

Organizer: Here, you will need a natural person or company that is actually filling out the form. This can only be you, another member of your company, or your attorney. You will also need this person's address. If this person is a natural person (not a company), you should sign as a natural person in the bottom. If this is a company, you'll sign as a company by putting the company name on top, your signature in the middle and printing your name below the signature with title. This signature area must match the section that requires the organizer's information, and they will get rejected if you list a natural person as organizer and sign as a company or vice versa.

Registered Agent: Your registered agent is responsible for receiving important documents from the state or potential claimants. This can be you, but whoever it is must be a resident or company physically located in this state and have an address that is not a PO box. Although a PO box might not be rejected, if someone isn't signing for certified mail or sheriff service of process, your company can be dissolved.

Principal Office: Your company is not required to have an office; however, if it does have a principal office, it should be recorded here. If you do not have an office, check the box that says this company does not have a principal office.

List of Company Officials. This is a section that I argued the Secretary of State include in their form, so I'm very happy it is listed now. It's important mostly for banks. Banks don't want to let just anyone open an account, so if you list someone as an officer on the articles themselves, a bank will accept that person's authority. They generally will accept an organizer's authority so long as that organizer is also a member.

Once you fill out all of the information, you'll need print this form off and sign is as the organizer. You will then scan this signed document in as a pdf and save to your computer in an area easy to remember.

Step 5: Sign up for an online account on North Carolina's Secretary of State page

Your articles can be mailed in, hand delivered, or submitted online. Hand delivery is the only way to get 4 hour return service; however, absent the need for extremely rapid turnaround, the best option, in my opinion, is online system. It costs $2, and allows you to make changes to the articles in case there are mistakes without having to wait for the returned mail. It is also very fast. If there isn't a backlog, you will typically receive a response within a few days. (No promise though, as the Secretary of State can take weeks to reply to your submission, if need be.) If you need rapid turnaround, the Secretary of State's website has a 24 hour turnaround for an extra $100.

To sign up for an account on the Secretary of State's website, first visit here:
http://www.sosnc.gov/corporations/

The form is simple:

E-Account Information

Is this a business entity: ⇩
[Yes ▾]

Entity Name:
[   ]

Address:
[   ]

City:	State:	Zip Code:	Country:
[ ]	[NC ▾]	[ ]	[USA ▾]

Telephone Number: ⇩
[   ]

Contact E-Mail: ⇩
[   ]

Notification E-Mail: ⇩
[   ]

Billing E-Mail: ⇩
[   ]

Account Name: ⇩
[   ]

Password: ⇩
[   ]

Verify Password: ⇩
[   ]

Industry: ⇩
[▾]

Enable ACH: ⇩
[No ▾]

Once you fill out the form and submit, you're automatically logged into your account. If you're logged out, you can log back in using the link in the upper right.

Step 6: Upload a Creation Filing

From here, you will go to "Upload a Creation Filing" on the left menu bar (pictured next page). This will bring you to another form to be filled out. This form requires you to include the new company's name, entity type, and document type. Your document type will be "Articles of Organization."

After inputting all of these fields, you must also upload the saved pdf of your signed articles by choosing the file and then clicking upload.

The next screen will show a list of the filings you have in process. You should only have one selection. Click on the radio button next to it, ensure the information in the following fields are correct and then click "Pay & Submit."

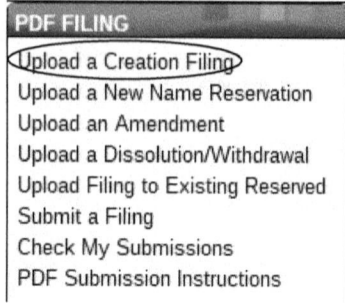

PDF FILING

Upload a Creation Filing
Upload a New Name Reservation
Upload an Amendment
Upload a Dissolution/Withdrawal
Upload Filing to Existing Reserved
Submit a Filing
Check My Submissions
PDF Submission Instructions

Step 7: Pay

On the payment page, you need to fill out the payment information and click through the page. Once payment is received and processed, you will reach the notification page. Then, you wait for the Secretary of State's office to accept or reject your articles.

Step 8: Make and Submit any Changes

If the articles are rejected, they will provide a reason. You will be able to make the necessary changes and resubmit the articles. Using the online system is best because you can email back and forth with the individual assigned to your filing until you have the articles of organization correct. Making corrections prior to your articles being approved costs you nothing extra. If, for whatever reason, you paid the wrong amount, you may have to pay the difference.

CHAPTER 5
STEPS AFTER ARTICLES
ARE APPROVED

Receiving your approved articles of organization or incorporation from the Secretary of State is a huge, tangible, first step to becoming a well-protected company. The next few steps are also very important.

EIN

The first step after approval is getting your Employer Identification Number (EIN). If you're obtaining this on your own behalf, you can do the entire process online and get your EIN in about 5 minutes. You will need your approved articles and personal information such as your social security number and address.

The EIN is your company's equivalent of a social security number. All the company's tax and banking records will be tied to this EIN. Every LLC and corporation needs an EIN regardless of if that company has employees.

We've create a nice walkthrough that you can use when completing your online EIN application. There is no charge, and the process is very quick. You do not need to pay someone to do this for you. We cover this portion in the next chapter.

Governing Document

Every LLC and Corporation is required to have a governing document; however, LLCs have a default one set by the North Carolina General Assembly. The terms North Carolina has set are fine for single member LLCs, but when you are operating a corporation or multimember LLC, you should create a governing document that meets your company's needs.

An LLC would have an operating agreement, which covers how the company is run and how the members interact with each other. Since an LLC is a collection of members, most of the document revolves around the members. We have information on this later in this book.

A corporation has bylaws. These are the rules that the management must follow when operating the business. A corporation is a separate legal entity and the delineation of duties are far more distinct than with an LLC. Because of this distinction, you see very little about owners' rights and responsibilities and more about management. Bylaws are usually accompanied by some form of equity agreement, stock purchase agreement, and/or stock plan to better define the owners' rights and responsibilities.

Your articles will always supersede your bylaws or operating agreement, so be sure to avoid conflicting with anything you put in your articles.

Bank Account

Every company should have its own bank account. Without a separate account, you risk personal liability for all the company's debts. That would defeat the purpose of setting up the company in the first place. Usually, a bank will need your approved articles, EIN, governing document, and identification in order to open your account. Our advice would be to use a bank that you trust, but it does not hurt to shop around for the bank that best serves your needs. A lot of banks have a free or cost effective account for very small companies.

Organization

Although you can always access your articles online at the Secretary of State's website, your approval cover page won't be available there. We recommend creating a place to store important records like your articles, EIN, bank account information, and your governing documents. Keeping all of this stuff in one place helps ensure you can access it when you need to. Always keep a backup!

Tax Elections

If you intend to be taxed differently than your organization's default type, you will have to make your tax election with the IRS as well. This occurs with corporations being taxed as S Corporations or LLCs electing to be taxed as any type of corporation. There may be limitations on when these elections can be made, so be sure to read the instructions or get help with them.

Licenses

To operate in North Carolina, your business will require certain licenses. Fortunately, North Carolina has a free service that you can call and gain all the information you need regarding which licenses you need for your location, industry, and what you provide. It is called the Business Link North Carolina (BLNC). To speak with a counselor, call 1-800-228-8443.

CHAPTER 6
OBTAIN AN EIN

After your articles of organization are accepted by the Secretary of State, the next step in the formation process is to apply for an employee identification number (EIN) from the IRS.

Obtaining an EIN is a fairly simple process that takes about 5 minutes to complete. The IRS has made a question and answer program on their site that guides you through the steps. Even though the process is so simple, don't rush through any parts because fixing an error after the fact is more difficult than applying for one in the first place.

The online application can be found here: http://www.irs.gov/Businesses/Small-Businesses-&-Self-Employed/Apply-for-an-Employer-Identification-Number-(EIN)-Online

Link to IRS EIN online application.

Note: Although it is online, the ability to file for an EIN is only available between the hours of 7am and 10pm Eastern time. Bizarre!

To begin, click the button at the bottom that reads Apply Online Now.

Step 1

The first thing the IRS needs to know is what type of business. We're forming a limited liability company in this guide. You should always select the correct type.

Step 2

The next page asks how many members and what state the LLC is located in. Answer these honestly. Entering incorrect information here can make problems for you, especially around tax time.

Note: In between many pages, there are pages that are informational in nature. You should read these to better understand the process and the requirements of having an EIN.

Step 3

The next input page asks why you need an EIN. Typically, this is because you've started a new business, but be sure to check the appropriate button.

Step 4

The next page asks about the responsible party. This is you if you're filing for your company's EIN. Go ahead and click individual to apply as a natural person. The next page will ask your personal information, name and social security number. It will also ask what makes you the responsible party. If you're not an owner, member, or manager, you are not the responsible party. You will have to do a few extra steps and are considered a third party designee. If you are a third party designee, you will also need an SS-4 and form 2848 on record in your files in case of audit

Step 5

The next step asks for information about the LLC's physical location. Even if the LLC does not have an office, you need to fill out this portion. You will likely have to use your home address or the address of your registered agent (if permissible by your agent) if you do not have a business address. The address you include here will not be publicly available. The IRS, however, will use it to contact the entity applying for the EIN.

Step 6

After that page, we finally get to the information on the LLC, like name and location. The IRS asks for state the company was formed as well as state the company is located. These can be different, so that's why both are asked.

Tip: You cannot include most punctuation marks in the name or address fields anywhere in this application.

Step 7

The next page contains what I refer to as the red flag items. Most companies will click 'no' for all of these, but be sure to read through them carefully. The final question on that page is asking about employees. If you're unsure whether you'll have employees in your first year, select 'no.' If you do end up hiring employees, you will need to make the appropriate filings with the IRS, but you will not be in any trouble.

Clicking yes on any of these may yield more work for you, but that shouldn't prevent you from receiving your EIN.

Step 8

The eighth page asks you to select what your business does. On most categories, there will be a subcategory on the following page as well. Select the category that best describes your business and move on. 'Other' is actually a very commonly used selection, so don't worry if you don't see something that fits exactly.

Tip: 'Service' is a subcategory of 'Other'.

Step 9

At this point, you're done inputting information. Just read through the next couple of pages and be sure to print off the confirmation letter that you receive, if you chose to receive it online.

Print off and download the pdf copy of the EIN. Keep these in a safe place. Requesting a new copy is a slower process that involves talking to the IRS. Note: If you were a third party designee, you will have to wait 4-8 weeks for this letter to arrive in the mail.

Errors

If you've done everything correctly, you'll likely have an EIN by the end of this process. If you receive an error, you should try a second time. If it still doesn't work, you should get help with this process.

Be sure to check the time if you receive an error. It may be too late to receive an EIN, even if they let you start the application. I wouldn't recommend starting an application after 9:45pm Eastern Time.

Tip: If you or someone previously registered a company with the same name in your state, you will have an error and have to call the IRS, even if that previous company is dissolved.

CHAPTER 7
WHAT'S IN AN OPERATING AGREEMENT

Operating agreements are the governing documents for limited liability companies. In these, you would specify the rights and responsibilities of the members of the company and how you want the company to be run. This is one of the most important documents you will have for your LLC, and a crucial one when there are multiple owners. As operating agreements tend to be less useful in single member LLCs, these next two chapters will focus on the most important considerations for a typical multi-member LLC.

This chapter will only outline the most common terms in an operating agreement, but the possibilities are endless. LLCs are incredibly flexible.

Keep in mind that companies vary wildly in their operation, so the things that are important to you might not be the same concerns others have. You want to be very thorough and cautious with your operating agreement. Mishaps in this document can cause very costly problems. Disputes between owners tend to be the costliest disputes a company can face.

Definitions

You've probably seen definitions in statutes, contracts, and all sorts of legal documents. An operating agreement is no different. Since it is such a powerful document, it is important that every member is clear on what a term means. An operating agreement is only as effective as it is clear to the members; therefore, your definitions section can be one of the more important sections of the agreement. It all depends on how you structure the agreement.

You'll see a pattern demanding clarity in each section. This can be accomplished in a number of ways. Improperly using a definitions section can make an operating agreement very unclear.

Member's Contributions

A section for handling member's contributions is important when considering profits and losses later on, as well as a place to illustrate how you value each member's contribution. Contributions can be labor, assets, cash, and promises. These contributions can be valued in any way that the agreement states. There are some separate rules when it comes to recognizing labor as a capital contribution for tax purposes, but that's not an issue for allocating profits and losses.

Membership Allocation

Membership allocation is where you determine who owns what share of the LLC. There are numerous ways you can divide up the company. What matters is having a clear method to determine how much each member owns and illustrating how much each will still have if additional members are added to the LLC at a later date.

Distributions of Profits and Losses

Your operating agreement may need a section that allocates profits and losses. Without this type of guidance in the operating agreement, division of profits is not as clear as it should be. Often times, the profits and losses are either divided equally amongst the members or divided based upon how much each member contributed.

The default rule for limited liability companies is that profits and losses are divided in proportion to the amount of ownership interest a person has in the LLC. There are many reasons why this doesn't make sense for your company. For example, if one of the members is a silent investor and invested in the company for 49% ownership yet should only receive 10% of the distributions, this needs to be specified in your operating agreement. It is in this portion you would also specify if and when members can receive salary for their labor contributions. Salary may, of course, be decided by management later on, but it's a far safer idea to make the decision in the operating agreement so that no one feels cheated by a later decision.

This section needs to be a combination of managing expectations and clearly stating exactly how payment works. If payment is based on percentage ownership, be sure to include, somewhere in the operating agreement, what labor or contribution requirements each member has. LLCs are very flexible and can divide profits and losses differently than from how ownership is divided. You can grant salaries, hourly wages, bonuses, prorated and non-prorated distributions, or any combination of these.

For example, you can give James a salary of $40,000 plus he receives 15% of any distribution made to the owners even though he owns 5% of the company. LLCs can do this. Corporations are a little different and since LLCs can be taxed as an S Corporation, you should be careful with distributions in unequal percentages from the ownership percentages if you're considering being taxed as an S Corp.

Taxation Options

There are numerous tax sections that can be utilized when starting a small business. In order to take advantage of these provisions, your company must sometimes elect to do so. Your operating agreement is where you can agree ahead of time what tax elections to make and who has the authority to make these elections.

A common example is if your LLC is to be taxed as an S Corporation, but not immediately. In that case, your members can agree when setting up that they'll elect that tax status upon a certain milestone. This is hugely beneficial if, in the future, a member is no longer as involved as he or she was.

Members Rights

Members need to know what their rights are, from voting rights to management rights. If it is clearly outlined in the operating agreement, it is less likely a member will overstep his or her authority and cause trouble for the LLC. Similarly, you should describe your member's duties. What each member is required to do as part of their membership should be clearly outlined. If one member is tasked with the technical side of a company and the other is in charge of the business side, this separation of duties should be explicit in the operating agreement.

Meetings

It is common to outline when and how meetings are held. This section is less important than the others, but can help with scheduling later. If the operating agreement specifies when meetings are, then the members were deemed to be on notice of potential decisions from the start. This can potentially save you from accusations that other members were not given an opportunity to have their voice heard on a particular matter.

In this section, you may also outline how voting works, what quorum is, what percent vote is needed to pass resolutions, and for the election of company officers. It is a good idea to have this portion very clear because this is a substantial right to most members in an LLC.

Record Keeping

Records are the memory of the company, so it is important to keep your records in a manner that others can comprehend. To do this, you need to be organized from the start. One good way of being organized is requiring general record keeping practices in your operating agreement. Getting audited is bad, but getting audited when you have poor record keeping methods could be incredibly costly.

Furthermore, NC law requires that every member have access to the books and records of the LLC. If you don't keep these books and records organized, you may be impeding on a member's guaranteed right.

Dissolution

Companies close down. It happens. When it does, it is important to have a plan in place on how to sell off or distribute assets to creditors and members. The last thing a failing company wants is to have the members suing each other.

Management

Management is one of the most important provisions from a legal standpoint. This is important to protect the company, all owners, and even third parties. It is protective because only those designated as management should have the authority to make decisions that bind the company. Banks especially want to see who has the authority to open bank accounts, sign contracts, and make decisions on behalf of the company. In your case, most often, you'll have one manager who has all the authority to bind the company. This manager can then delegate responsibilities to those below him or her. The manager is president of the company. He has all of the authority, but will likely need to hire others to run certain aspects of the company. Using contract law, these lower level managers can make their position fairly secure, but initially, the manager has the authority to change their powers in any way, including firing them. In most LLCs, the management is elected by the owners; however, the actual process for choosing management must be defined in your operating agreement.

The more complicated way to do management is to separate different areas of authority in the operating agreement itself. For example, you can have an operations manager, marketing manager and executive manager, each with his or her own powers and limitations. The part that makes this more complicated is that you must be sufficiently detailed enough that there's no gaps in authority (things the company needs done that no manager has the authority to do), and limited number of overlaps (things that multiple managers would be able to make the decision on). Either failing to cover all management aspects or having overlap between managers can create large issues within the company, and this needs to be carefully construed to avoid those. I've seen many companies have struggles resulting from an overly complex management structure.

Disagreements

Owners disagree. It happens to every company, no matter how close the owners are. The important thing is to ensure that when the disagreements come up, there are clear rules in your operating agreement as to how to deal with them. These rules can vary wildly ranging from a coin flip to a forced sale of the company. It is imperative that the way the disagreement is settled is fair. To be fair, it must be clearly outlined and it must be established prior to any disagreement or ill will. If the policy is unfair, ambiguous, or created after disagreements start, it may actually lead to larger problems than just the disagreement.

The key is to agree on these policies when the waters are calm. Once the waters are choppy, the disagreement provisions are important, but agreeing on them without a mediator will be difficult and can lead to larger problems.

Determining whether to use mediation, arbitration, neither, or both is something you should decide up front. Mediation can be helpful for finding a quicker and usually less costly resolution, but it is never fully binding. Arbitration can be binding. Without a binding resolution process, any member can take a dispute to court, and that can be a very lengthy process. There are pros and cons to every approach, so there is no way to recommend one over the other without knowing your situation and desired company culture.

Operating Agreement Changes

Even though the goal is to create an operating agreement that fits every situation in the company every time, that's simply not possible. Therefore, you need to have a clear mechanism for how the operating agreement may be changed. A two thirds majority vote of all members is a fairly common way to do it; however, you may want to look closely at who, if anybody, would be harmed with this approach. Try to find a mechanism that is fair and balanced for majority and minority members.

Sometimes, it is a good idea to require not only a percentage vote, but also a certain number of members. If one member owns 75% of the company, under the straight percentages approach, he or she could change the operating agreement unilaterally. Therefore, requiring either 76% of the vote or 66% of the vote plus requiring at least two people to agree would be a good way to ensure that he or she has the most say, but cannot make any changes on his or her own.

Even with this provision clearly spelling out how the operating agreement may be changed, courts have held that there are limits to what may be changed. If you think about it, this makes sense. It would be clearly unfair if you could amend the operating agreement to specify that another member's (who we'll call Joel) membership interest is now worth $0 and that the company has the authority to buy him out at any time at that price. If Joel was a minority member who couldn't materially impact the vote to change the operating agreement, he could be removed through this process, and therefore, the courts can step in to protect him.

Additionally, certain changes will be invalid. The law guarantees certain rights, so any limitations to these guaranteed rights would be invalid.

How to add members?

Outlining how new members can be added is a very important part of your operating agreement. By default, every time you add a new member to the LLC, you dilute the ownership interest of every other member. Without specific rules as to how members are added, you could harm minority members in the company without their prior knowledge or counsel.

For example, you can admit new members with 2/3rd majority vote, as long as all the members agreed to this prior to joining the company. There are legal rights of minority members to protect them from getting abused by majority members in a company. Without these protective rules, a majority member could just keep issuing himself new ownership in the company, or give ownership to family and friends who do not have the same ideals as the minority member.

One way to ensure everyone is protected is to require a buy-in for all new members at fair market value. This way, even though a member's percentage ownership may decrease, the value will remain the same.

For example, let's say a member owns 10 shares of a 100 share company and the company is worth $100. If a new member joins and receives 10 shares for $10, the overall value of the company is worth $110. This still leaves the original member's shares worth $10 total.

Despite the above example, there can still be lost value if a member loses some level of control over the company. These concerns will also need to be addressed if they're important to any member.

Buyout Provisions?

Especially when there's one more powerful member, there should be clear limitations on how the company or the majority member may remove other members, if that power is granted at all. Sometimes, these provisions are called "forced buy out provisions," but by any name, they're provisions that allow one member or the company as a whole to buy back or force a member to surrender all of their ownership interest.

Like many of the other areas of the operating agreement, you must ensure the provision you create is enforceable. Fairness is actually very important here. Courts are hesitant to agree with a company that makes a wholly one sided buyout clause, especially if the courts can find that the clause was unclear or that the exiting member was not fully aware of what this provision meant. If the provision made the operating agreement illusory (where one side can choose who has to follow the rules), it will likely be unenforceable.

Additionally, you need to be careful with these provisions, as they're a huge source of conflict. If you're forcing someone to leave the company against their will, there's a high chance this person will sue. These lawsuits can be incredibly expensive because it's a fairly technical and very valuable conflict. The valuation in the forced buyout may vary millions of dollars, and that is worth fighting over.

Removal

There are many legitimate reasons you'll need to have a provision that allows the removal of a member. For example, if a member is required to contribute 40 hours per week to the company and does not, there needs to be available recourse to protect the company and the other members.

Some operating agreements have "morality clauses" that allow for the removal of a member for moral reasons. These clauses can be good or bad. The most important thing is that they're clear and fair to all members.

How can a member leave?

It's important to have a plan in place for when members leave. Your operating agreement should place conditions on when a member may leave, what rights and responsibilities a departing member has and what the company must do in that event.

Under the default rules in North Carolina, a member may leave whenever he or she wants and can either keep or disown the ownership in the LLC. That member may also sell or transfer his or her ownership to any person or company at any time and may delegate any of his or her rights and responsibilities to any person who is otherwise lawfully able to take on those rights and responsibilities. That's a plethora of open-ended options!

If you don't like those default rules (which most people don't), your operating agreement must change them. This is an area where you will need to be very specific. For example, if you have a provision that disallows a departing member from collecting equity distributions without contributing a certain amount of labor, make that clear in case that departing member wants to fight the provision in court. Any time a person is required to give up something of value, you will be facing a potential lawsuit. The more specific these rules, the easier it will be for a court to rule in your favor. Clarity also deters lawsuits.

In this section, it is vital that you do not try to get too creative. Creativity here often creates confusion and mistakes. If you're doing anything overly complicated, you should seek out the assistance of an attorney.

Requirements of Membership

In your operating agreement, you can specify requirements for your members. For example, you can require that members contribute labor, money, intellectual property, or other forms of property. You can also require certain things such as a non-compete, non-disclosure, and morality requirements for your members. These duties may be different for different members. To illustrate this, you are able to require that Aaron contributes 30 hours of work every week and sign a non-disclosure agreement, whereas Tammy has to contribute her patents and not compete against the company for the time she is member and several years afterwards.

Your requirements can be very expansive as long as they're agreed to by the members. Obviously, you cannot change the requirements after the fact unless agreed to by the member who is being affected. Your requirements also cannot be against public policy. In other words, you cannot force a member to commit a crime, perpetrate a fraud, or anything similar. If you do, that member may ignore those requirements and depending on the remainder of the agreement, he or she will likely still be entitled to the membership interest.

Transfers of Membership interest

Membership interest is personal property. By default, it can be bought, sold, traded, gifted, etc in any manner that a piece of furniture would be able to. You can even use your membership interest as collateral for a loan, or have a lien attached to it as a result of a judgment. The unique aspect of LLC ownership in North Carolina is that only the economic interest (aka "profits interest") may be taken by creditors. The creditors can receive a "charging order." This means they are entitled to any income that passes down from the company to your interest. You maintain the management and ownership interest.

For voluntary transfers (when you sell or gift your ownership interest), you're entitled to transfer the whole membership interest or any part of it. You can set up reasonable restrictions on the transfer of membership interest.

Operating agreements usually limit the ability to transfer ownership. This limitation helps prevent gaining unwanted owners that can negatively impact the company. From my experience, I've found that most people like to generally limit the ability to transfer ownership and create preemptive rights when a member passes away, files for bankruptcy, and many other situations where an owner may lose ownership.

This is also the portion of the operating agreement where you can determine the value of company to use in case of litigation or forced buyouts.

Right of First Refusal: The right of first refusal is something you can include in your agreement. It is a right granted to other members or the company to be the first to purchase the membership interest, at the same predefined terms, if one member chooses to sell or otherwise transfer his or her interest. What this means is that if James tries to sell his membership interest to Sara for $10,000, either the company or other members may step in and purchase the membership interest for $10,000 from James. Determining who is granted this right of first refusal is subject to the terms of the operating agreement.

Courts are reluctant to uphold a provision that is an absolute restriction on the transfer of membership interest unless there's a legitimate business interest in doing so. For example, an absolute restriction on transferring units during a period of sales negotiation might be enforceable because it keeps the value of the company higher and prevents insider trading. A restriction that prevents a member from transferring his or her shares indefinitely without reason would almost certainly be held unenforceable because it would be what's referred to as an "unreasonable restraint on alienation" of the membership interest.

Restrictions on the sale or transfer is a balancing act between your desire to protect your business from outsiders and the unreasonable restraint on the alienation of the membership interest. There are many legitimate business reasons, so don't let this scare you. In personal services LLCs, replacing one professional for another may not be an equal trade, so preventing this would likely be a legitimate interest.

Membership interest can also be transferred involuntarily through death, bankruptcy, an owner's dissolution, receivership, and other situations where someone is appointed to handle all, or most, of your property on your behalf. These are areas where you have to specifically address what happens. If you have the company buy the membership interest back at a reasonable price, the creditors or heirs on the other side will likely prefer this option, as they will no longer be tasked with trying to sell the property on their own. The key is determining what is fair to avoid costly conflict.

What happens when a member dies?

Unfortunately, people die and many times you cannot predict when this happens. As much of the operating agreement's role is to eliminate unpredictability, you need to address what happens if a member dies. You should not only address what happens with his or her membership units, but also what happens to his or her rights and responsibilities under the operating agreement. For example, if the member was required to contribute 40 hours of labor every week to the company, how will this value be replaced?

If a member offers something of great value to the company, you should consider life insurnace. That way, you can replace his or her contribution with a salaried employee or restructure to meet the new circumstances.

CHAPTER 8
CHECK MARK STARTUP

Starting Your North Carolina LLC was very narrowly tailored to forming an LLC in North Carolina. Although it contained a lot of great information about that process, this is only a tiny fraction of the things you need to consider when starting your own business.

Check Mark Startup is a fantastic book by Richard Wayne Bobholz about taking your values and an idea and turning it into a strong business. The process can take as little as a week and saves business owners time, money, and stress while ensuring their business is on a solid legal and business foundation.

The real beauty of Check Mark Startup is the simplicity of each step. Richard requires the reader to know very little about business or law in order to jump in and create their own business from scratch. Built for beginners and experts alike, this book is a must have for any entrepreneur.

By the end of the book, you will have a working company, contracts, and many

other business and legal documents customized for your company's needs. To find out more and get special tips, tricks, and promotions, check out www.checkmarkstartup.com or buy it on Amazon.

ABOUT THE AUTHOR

Richard Bobholz is an award-winning attorney, speaker, business owner, teacher, and dedicated community member. He is the author of several other books in the business and science fiction genres, focusing his more recent publications on business, legal, and computer programming. Beyond helping his community through these resources, Richard dedicates a significant amount of his time to providing community service and pro bono legal services to the less fortunate in his community.

Richard enjoys running, backpacking, computer programming, writing, and spending time with family and friends.

Richard obtained his Bachelor's Degree in Economics at Michigan Technological University and his Juris Doctorate from the Kline School of Law at Drexel University.

Richard currently practices at Law Plus Plus, a revolutionary and award-winning law firm that is dedicated to making the legal system easier, enacting positive change in the community, and constantly improving how they operate and the effect they have on their clients' lives and in their profession. With this mission and his genuine approach to the practice of law, he is able to help small businesses, nonprofits, and social entrepreneurs protect themselves and develop their businesses in a deliberate and systematic manner.

Above the degrees and accolades, Richard values his ability to see things from multiple perspectives. This view of the world helps him break down problems into their simplest components and build a solution from that analysis. It is this style of thinking that allows him to create such useful books and guides, and is an incredibly valuable resource for his clients.

In 2015, Law Plus Plus was recognized by the American Bar Association for their contribution to pro bono services, taking second place nationwide for their commitment, and in 2016, Law Plus Plus became the first law firm in North Carolina to become B Corporation Certified.

Beyond those accomplishments, the attorneys at Law Plus Plus also contribute hundreds of hours every year toward community service through programs like Habitat for Humanity, Clean Jordan Lake, the Food Bank, Activate Good and so many more.

Richard also sits on the Board of Directors for Activate Good, an amazing organization that promotes and pairs volunteers with causes, creating a multiplier effect in the community.

Flat Rate Prices

www.lawplusplus.com/easyfee/easyfee-business

Law Plus Plus offers almost exclusively flat rate prices. They can be found at the above link or by scanning this QR Code.

Contact
Richard Bobholz
richard@lawplusplus.com
919-912-9640